EXPERIMENTS
with
LIGHT

LEARNERS

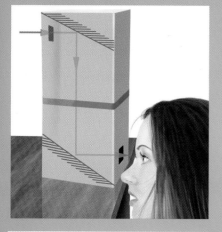

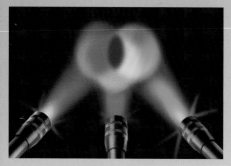

Contents

What Is Light?

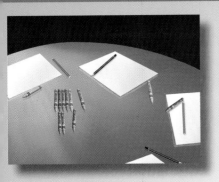

Light is a messenger that tells us about our surroundings. It is a form of energy. Light helps us to (see shapes and colours.)
What would happen if there was no light? Let us check.

You will need:

- friends
- a piece of paper for each friend
- a set of crayons for each
- a pencil for each

1. Sit down in a room with your friends. Each one should have a set of paper, pencil and crayons.
2. Draw this picture on your sheet.
3. Put the lights off and if required draw the curtains and close the doors to make the room dark.
4. Now try to colour the picture.
5. After 10 minutes or so, put the lights on.
6. Check how each one of you has fared! Do you think you could have done a better job if the lights were on? Why? (By the way, how did you check the time?)

Without light

- you would not know where you are, or
- where your table tennis racket is, or for that matter,
- whether it is time to play or time to study, or
- watch your favourite TV programme!

Life surely would be boring, wouldn't it?

Without light, life would not just be boring, it would be impossible.

The sun gives us natural light. Sun light helps green plants make their food. Without light, green plants would not grow and there would be no food, and so, no life...

Green magic

You will need:

- 3 pieces of cardboard
- 4 paper clips
- a patch of grass
- a plant with big leaves
- a rock or brick

1. Choose a corner of a lawn. Put one cardboard on a patch of grass. Put the brick or rock on the cardboard so that it is not blown away.
2. Put the other two cardboards, one over, and the other under a large leaf, so that a part of the leaf is covered. Clip the cardboards together as shown. Then put the plant in a sunny spot.
3. Leave the cardboards for 2-3 days. Then remove them. Is there any change in the grass or the leaf?
4. Check the patch of grass and the leaf everyday. How long does it take to get back the green colour?

Try this

Tigers do not eat greens. How is it that tigers too die of hunger if plants do not grow?

Sources of Light

Light makes it possible for us to see. We can see a bulb because it gives off light. A bulb is a source of light. But all things around us do not give off their own light. We are able to see these things because light shines on them and then bounces back into our eyes. How many sources of light can you spot in this picture? List them.

Natural sources of light

The most important source of light on earth is the sun. The light from the sun travels through space at an incredible speed of 1,86,000 miles per second and reaches the earth in 8 minutes. Fast indeed! Just think, the fastest moving aeroplane would take a little more than three and a half years to make the trip!

Ans: table lamp, candle, sun, fireplace, stars, lamps.

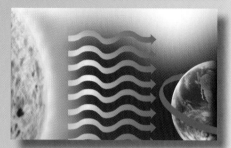

When the sun sets, day turns into night and it becomes dark. The night sky has the moon and innumerable stars. However, despite their brightness the moon and the stars can hardly keep the darkness away. The moon actually has no light of its own. It reflects the light of the sun. The stars on the other hand give off their own light. But they are too far away from the earth. So very little of their light reaches us.

Did you know that the sun is also a star? It is the nearest star. That is why it looks so bright and big compared to other stars.

Artificial sources of light

Man has made artificial sources of light so that he could see and work in the dark. The first man-made light was fire. Then he learnt the use of oil lamps, candles and gaslights. Now most artificial lighting is done through electricity. Let us go on a light hunt.

You will need:

- a piece of paper
- a pen or a pencil

1. Look at the picture below and point out the sources of light you see.
2. List out the ones which are artificial sources of light.

Try this

Do all the light sources you have listed, give out heat? Find out if there is any relation between heat and light?

Ans: Artificial sources: Lamp, Torch, Neon Light, Traffic-lights, Streetlight

The Path of Light

How does light travel from one place to another? Can we see the path of light? Let us try.

You will need:

- a torch
- a duster or a small rug

1. In a darkened room, keep the torch on a table and focus the beam on a wall. Can you see the beam of light between the torch and the wall? Probably you can only see the light coming out of the torch and a patch of light on the wall.
2. Now, beat the duster or rug so that dust flies into the air between the torch and the wall. Can you see the beam?

The path of light can be seen when there is dust, smoke or fog (water droplets) in the path of the beam. These tiny particles reflect light into our eyes and show us the passage of light.

While studying the path of light did you notice the edges of the beam? Was it straight or curved? Mark the correct picture.

Light travels in straight lines. Light normally cannot bend or turn around corners. Let us check.

You will need:

- an empty cardboard box or carton
- a knitting needle or a straight thin rod
- a candle
- a matchbox

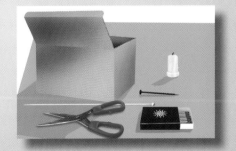

1. Cut out the top of the box.
2. Pass the knitting needle through the two facing sides of the carton. Remove the needle. Now there will be two holes on the two sides.
3. Place the box on a table. Light the candle. Fix the candle near one hole. The flame should be at about the same height as the hole.
4. Look through the other hole. Can you see the flame?
5. Cut out a strip from the lid of the carton. Insert it in the box between the two holes.
6. Look through the hole again. Can you still see the flame?

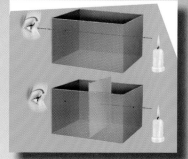

The cardboard insert blocked the straight path of light. If light from the candle could bend around, you could have seen the flame.

But why did light not pass through the cardboard that was inserted?
Light cannot pass through everything. When light falls on an object, a part of it bounces back from the surface, a part passes through it, and the rest of the light gets absorbed by the object. This is true for all things, be it solid, liquid or gas. Let us check it out.

You will need:

- objects of daily use
- a pen or a pencil
- a torch or a bulb

1. Hold each item in front of a lighted torch or bulb and try to see the light through it.
2. The table given below has three columns. List the items in the correct columns depending upon what you saw.

Can see clearly	Can see partly	Cannot see
These items that allow light to pass are *Transparent.*	These items that scatter light are *Translucent.*	These items that do not allow light to pass are *Opaque.*

Light and Shadows

You will need:

- a bright source of light
- a wall

1. In a darkened room, hold your hand in between the source of light and the wall. What do you see?
   What you see on the wall is the shadow of your hand.
2. Move your hand closer to the wall. Is there any change in the size of the shadow? What happens if there are two lights in the room?
3. Try forming shadows with other things.

Why are shadows formed?

Your hand is opaque. So light from the bulb could not pass through it. Neither could it bend round your hand. So the part of the wall which did not get any light due to your hand, remained dark. This formed the shadow in the shape of your hand.

Try this

Do transparent and translucent objects have shadows?
Try to find out.

Shadow puppet

You will need:

- a thin card
- a pencil
- a pair of scissors
- a torch
- a needle and thread
- a broomstick
- glue

1. Draw the body of the puppet on the card. Draw the head, arms and legs separately. Cut out the pieces.
2. Stitch the arms, legs and head to the body loosely so that they turn freely. You can also use small pins or brass paper fasteners.
3. Stick the broomstick to the back of the puppet. Hold it in front of a wall and shine the torch on it. Shake the broomstick and move the puppet.
4. Watch its shadow dance!

Changing shadows

The shapes and sizes of shadows depend on the postition and distance of the source of light from the object. Let us do an outdoor experiment.

You will need:

- a pole or a tree
- a rope
- a measuring tape
- a nail or a brick to make scratches on the ground
- a watch
- papers and a pen or a pencil

1. On a sunny day at about 8 am, go out and find an isolated tree in the garden. Can you see the shadow of the tree?
2. Mark the position of the shadow with the nail. Measure its length with the help of the rope and the measuring tape. Note it down. Also note the time on your watch.
3. At intervals of two hours (ie, 10 am, 12 noon, 2 pm and 4 pm) go out and repeat step 2.

Is the shadow changing its position with time?
What about the length of the shadow?

4. By looking at the shadows of the tree in the pictures given below, can you tell the time?

Eclipse

The earth travels around the sun while the moon moves around the earth. In the course of their movement it sometimes so happens that the earth, the moon and the sun come in a straight line. When the moon comes beween the sun and the earth, it casts a shadow on the earth. So the sun gets out of view, or is eclipsed, from some part of the earth. This is called a Solar Eclipse. The centre of the shadow receives no light from the sun and the eclipse there is total. At the edges of the shadow some light can reach the earth and the eclipse is partial.

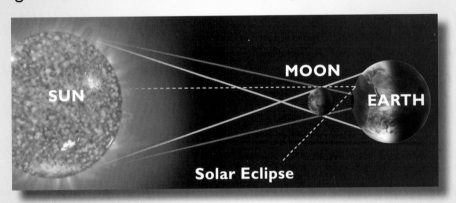

When the earth comes between the sun and the moon, the earth casts its shadow on the moon. The moon then becomes invisible at places where the shadow falls on it and it is called the eclipse of the moon or a Lunar Eclipse. Have you seen a lunar eclipse? Can you label this picture of a lunar eclipse? Shade the area on earth from which the moon cannot be seen. Take help from the picture above and from what you have read so far.

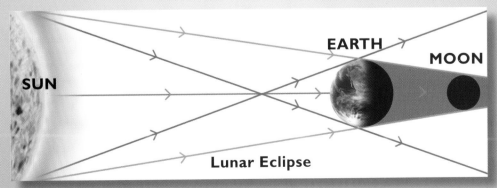

Reflected Light

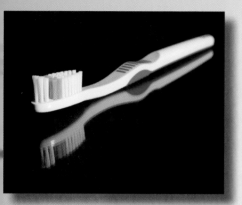

Most things bounce or reflect light. Polished or shiny surfaces reflect most of the light that falls on them. They are good reflectors. You can see clear reflections in a shiny metal sheet, a glass table or still water.

Look at the water in a pond or a lake. If there is no wind and the water is still, you can see reflections of the trees, people and other things around it.

Try this

Is there any problem with the reflected images? Why does everything look upturned?

Mirrors

A mirror is usually a flat sheet of glass with a thin layer of a shiny metal such as silver or aluminium behind the glass. Mirrors are very good reflectors. They are specially designed to reflect light so as to form exact images. However, an object seen in a mirror seems to be turned around. The left and the right get interchanged. Let us check this.

You will need:

• A large mirror

1. Stand in front of the mirror and smile at your mirror image. The image smiles back.
2. Now wave at your image with your right hand. What does the image do?

Secret Code

This sidewise inversion of mirror images can be used to design a secret code among friends.

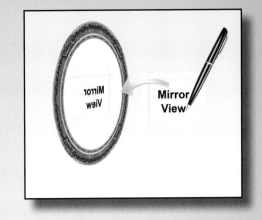

You will need:

- a mirror that stands upright
- pieces of paper
- a pen or a pencil

1. Write your name or any simple word on a piece of paper.
2. Place the mirror next to the paper. Can you read the image?
3. Now by looking at the mirror, copy the reversed letters on another piece of paper.
4. Practise this till you can write small words and your name without the help of a mirror.
5. Use this as a secret code to communicate among friends. To decode the message, hold it before a mirror.

Periscope

A periscope uses mirror reflections to help you see around solid objects. Submarines use periscopes to keep watch on enemy ships while remaining under water.

Make your own periscope

You will need:

- 2 litres cartons (oil, milk, tea etc., come in cardboard cartons)
- 2 small mirrors
- a pair of scissors
- sellotape

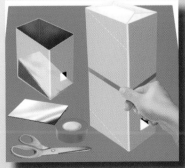

1. Cut off the tops of both the cartons. About an inch from the bottom of each carton, cut out a one-inch square hole.
2. Place the mirrors diagonally at the bottom of the two cartons as shown. The mirrors should face the holes. Adjust the mirrors in the cartons so that they are at almost the same slope. Tape the mirrors in place.

3. Place the cartons, one on top of the other. The cut out holes should be on opposite sides. Tape the cartons together.
4. Now stand behind a boundary wall. Hold the periscope so that the top hole is above the wall while the bottom hole is below it. See through the bottom hole. Can you see what is on the other side of the wall?

How does a periscope work?

Light from the object gets reflected on the top mirror, falls on the bottom one, gets reflected again and reaches your eyes. So you are actually looking at a reflection of a reflection!

Make a kaleidoscope

You will need:

- 2 long, narrow mirrors
- a card
- sellotape
- paper
- oil
- coloured marble paper
- a torch

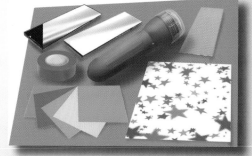

1. Tape the mirrors together along the long side.
2. Now tape between them a piece of card, the same size as the mirrors, so that you get a triangular shape.
3. Cover one end with a piece of paper and tape it. Smear the paper with a little oil and let it dry.
4. Now cut tiny pieces of the coloured sheets of paper and put them in the tube.
5. Make a small hole in another piece of paper. Cover the top of the tube with it and tape it as shown. Your kaleidoscope is ready.

6. Shine a torch through the oiled side of the paper, and look through the hole. Can you see colour patterns? Shake the kaleidoscope. What do you see?

Concave and convex mirrors

Some mirrors are designed in special ways. *Concave mirrors* make the image look bigger than the object. They curve away from the viewer. *Convex mirrors* make the image look smaller than the size of the object. They are curved towards the viewer.

Have you seen concave and convex mirrors? Check the driver's mirror and the side-mirror in a car. What about the headlight of a car?

Fun with reflectors

Concave and convex reflectors can make you look pulled out and thin or squat and fat. Let us see.

You will need:

- a steel glass
- a big metal spoon
- a flexible tin plate

1. Look at yourself in the steel glass. What do you notice? Is the glass surface concave or convex?
2. Look at your reflection in the spoon from both sides. Are the reflections like what you expected?
3. Hold the tin plate carefully by the sides. You should be able to see your own reflection.
4. Bend the sheet once towards you, and then slowly away from you. What happens?

Refraction

Normally, light travels unbothered in straight lines. But when it passes from one transparent thing to another, say from air to water or glass, light rays get bent at the surface between the two things. Light, coming through water in a glass, is bent right at the surface of the water. But once light enters air, it again travels in straight lines. This phenomenon is called the refraction of light.

Let us check this.

You will need:

- a glass of water
- a pencil

1. Put the pencil in the glass of water so that it is partly under water.
2. Look at the pencil from the top of the glass. What has happened to the pencil? Does it look bent at the water surface?
3. Do you notice any difference if you look from the side?
4. Take the pencil out of the water. Does it still look broken?

There is nothing wrong with the pencil. What happens is that the light rays from the part of the pencil under water bend, as they pass through air before reaching your eyes. Your eyes mistake it for the bending of the pencil.

A Kingfisher sees a fish. Due to refraction, he thinks that the fish is further away from the bank than where it actually is. What does the fish see?

An illusion

You will need:

- water
- a tumbler (opaque)
- a coin
- sellotape
- a friend

1. Tape the coin to the bottom of the tumbler.
2. Place your eyes so that the coin is just out of view.
3. Ask the friend to pour water in the tumbler.
4. What do you see?

Lenses

A lens bends light in such a way that objects viewed through it look larger or smaller. Lenses are usually made of glass. A convex lens can make objects look larger than they actually are. It is thicker at the centre than at the edges. A concave lens is thicker at the sides than at the centre. The image formed by a concave lens is smaller in size than the object.

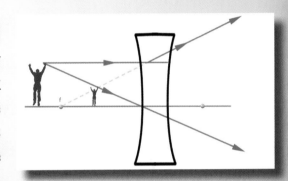

Have you seen concave and convex lenses? I am sure you have. Check it out.

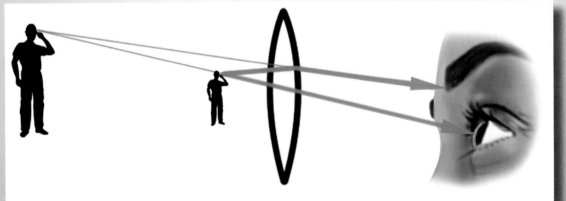

1. With the permission of the owner of the spectacles, touch the glasses and feel the curvature. Are the glasses convex or concave?
People who cannot see nearby things need convex lenses to see properly. Those who cannot see faraway things use concave lenses.

Did you know that your eye is a lens?

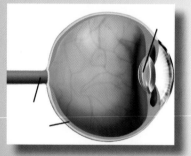

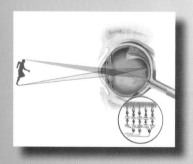

How do you see things? Light, after bouncing or bending from objects, enters your eyes through a tiny round black hole in your eye. It is called the *pupil*. Look at the dark-coloured circle in your eye. It is the *iris*. If you look carefully, you will find the black round pupil inside the iris.

When light falls in your eye, the pupil widens or narrows to let the right amount of light in. This light falls on the convex lens inside your eye. The lens focuses the light on the back of the eye, which is called the *retina*. The retina is like a screen. Images of things you look at are formed there. These images are then sent to the brain.

If your eyes fail to focus light on the retina, you see hazy images. Depending on whether your eyes focus before or beyond the retina, you need a concave lens or a convex lens.

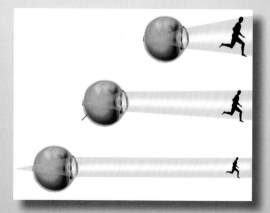

A *magnifying glass* is a convex lens that magnifies or increases the size of things, when viewed through it. A magnifying glass of power 4 simply means that things will appear 4 times bigger in size when viewed through it. Get a magnifying glass. Toy shops keep magnifying glasses. Otherwise get it from a shop that sells scientific instruments.

Hold the glass near this page. How do the letters look? Take it outside, and view leaves and small insects through it.
As you look at your insect specimens, guess what they see?
A giant eye, since the lens acts both ways.

Make your own magnifier

You can make a magnifier out of a water droplet.

You will need:

- a cardboard
- a 50p coin
- a pencil
- a pair of scissors
- a dropper or a drinking straw
- water

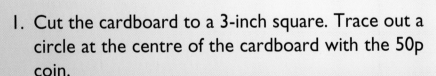

1. Cut the cardboard to a 3-inch square. Trace out a circle at the centre of the cardboard with the 50p coin.
2. Cut out the circle. Put sellotape over the hole.
3. Using the dropper, carefully put a drop of water onto the tape. The water should form a small round lens.
4. Put your lens over a leaf. What do you see?

Study other small things with it.

Can you see the cells of a leaf with your magnifier? Very minute things like leaf cells, body cells, bacteria etc., cannot be seen even through a magnifying glass. *Microscopes* are used to study such things. A microscope has two convex lenses that can magnify tiny objects many hundred times!

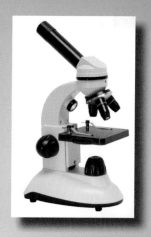

What do you think this picture is of?
Did you say forest? Sorry, it is a picture of two healthy human hairs growing from a clean scalp as seen through a very powerful microscope.

A pair of convex lenses are also used to study very far-away and distant objects like the moon and the stars. The instrument used for this purpose is called an *astronomical telescope*.

Telescopes with two convex lenses are however unsuitable for land viewing because they give inverted images. A pair of convex and concave lenses is used to see distant objects, like hill tops. It is called a *terrestrial telescope*. *Binoculars* have two such telescopes. Have you seen far-away things with a pair of binoculars?

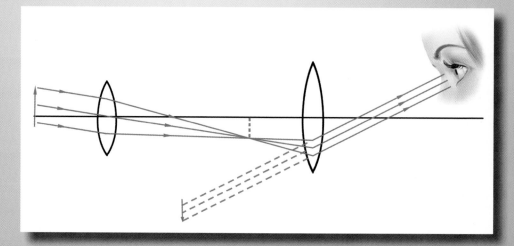

The Colour of Light

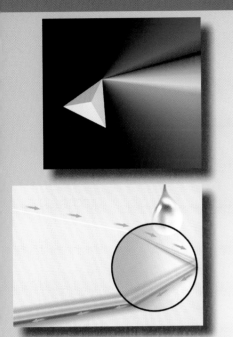

Light from the sun and from ordinary electric bulbs is called white light. White light is made of seven colours: violet, indigo, blue, green, yellow, orange and red. This band of colours is called the spectrum.

A *prism* is a specially cut piece of glass that can split white light into the colours of the spectrum. When white light falls on a prism, each colour gets bent a little differently. The violet end of the spectrum is bent more than the red end. The result is a separation of the colours.

Raindrops act like tiny prisms. When the sun shines during rainfall, the raindrops bend the light and break it up into its seven colours. This forms *a rainbow*. Have you seen a rainbow?

Create your own rainbow

You will need:

- a glass
- water
- a large piece of paper

1. Choose a window from which sunlight is entering the room.
2. Place the glass on the window sill. Fill the glass to the brim with water. See that light falls on the water.
3. Place the white paper on the floor and receive the light refracted from the water. Can you see the rainbow colours? Which colour forms the outer-most band?

Colours in bubbles

You will need:
- a detergent soap solution
- a wire

1. Bend the wire into a circle to form a loop.
2. Dip the loop in the detergent solution and blow. You will form bubbles. Do the experiment outdoors, on a sunny day.
3. Can you see any colour on the bubbles?

Primary colours

Red, green and blue are the main colours that constitute light. These are known as primary colours. We can get white light by mixing red, blue and green lights. All other colours can be made by mixing these colours in different amounts. The colours you get when you mix two primary colours, are called secondary colours. These are, magenta, which is got by a combination of red and blue lights; cyan, a combination of green and blue lights and yellow, a combination of red and green lights. Did you expect the red and green lights to give a yellow light?

Remember that mixing lights is not the same as mixing colour paints. Let us check this.

You will need:
- 3 torch lights
- red, blue and green cellophane paper
- rubber bands
- a paint box and a brush

1. Fix the three-coloured cellophane papers to the three torches with rubber bands.
2. Make the room dark. Take the blue and green torches and focus the beams on the wall so that parts of the beams overlap. What colour is the overlapped area?
3. Repeat this with other combinations. Note what you see.
4. Focus all the three torches and see the resultant overlap. Is it almost white?
5. Now mix blue, red and green paints. What colour do you get?

Did you guess that the idea of getting all colours from three colours is used in the making of colour pictures in television sets?

Colour wheel

You will need:

- cards
- a compass
- a pencil
- a paint box and a brush
- glue
- toothpicks

1. Draw and cut out circles of a card. Divide the circles into 4 sections and colour the sections red and green alternately.
2. Push a toothpick through the centre of the circle and fix it with glue.
3. Spin the wheel. What colour do you see?
4. Similarly make wheels with blue and red, blue and green and blue, red and green. Spin to see the effect.
5. Now make a wheel with the colours of the spectrum. You can leave out indigo. Dividing a circle into 12 sections is easier. Spin the wheel and see what happens.

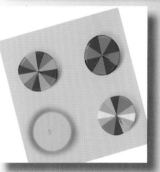
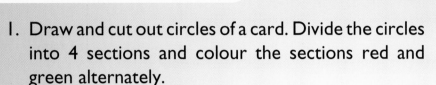

The colour of objects

Why does a red rose look red?

When light falls on any object, we have learnt that a part of the light is either reflected or passed through, while a part is absorbed. When white light falls on a red object, all colours of the white light get absorbed, except red. The red light reflects and reaches your eyes. So the object appears red. This is true for all coloured things.

Think this over

What about black objects? When do things appear black?

Did you guess that the colour of an object will depend on the colour of the light in which the object is seen? Let us check this.

- a pencil
- white paper
- red and green crayons
- red cellophane paper
- a torch

1. On the white piece of paper draw a picture of the rose as shown, and colour it red. Make the leaves green.
2. Cover the torch with the red cellophane paper.
3. Focus the red torchlight on your picture. How does the picure look?

What happens is that when seen in red light, both the white paper and the red rose on it reflect the red light. So the rose merges with the background and you see a faint outline. On the other hand the green leaves absorb the red light, and no light is reflected to your eyes. So the green leaves appear black.

Colour filters

A colour filter is a transparent piece of coloured glass, plastic or paper that allows light of a particular colour to pass through it. It blocks or filters out other colours. Colour filters are used in stage lighting and photography.

Make your own colour filters

You will need:

- a cardboard
- coloured cellophane papers (green, red, blue and yellow)
- a pair of scissors
- glue
- a pen or a pencil

1. Cut out four cards of 4-inch squares from the cardboard. Draw a 3-inch square inside each cardboard square and cut along the lines. You get 4 cardboard frames.
2. Cut out 4-inch squares from green, red, blue and yellow cellophane papers and paste them on the cardboard frames. Your green, red, blue and yellow filters are ready.
3. Go out in the sun and choose a colourful object. Notice the different colours.
4. Now hold the red filter in front of your eyes. What do you notice? Does the object appear in shades of red and black?

5. While seeing the object through the red filter, bring in the green filter between your eyes and the red filter. What happens? Can the red light from the red filter still enter your eyes?

6. Repeat steps 4 and 5 with other colours. What colours do the yellow filters pass? Remember that yellow light is a combination of red and green lights.

How do your eyes see colours?

Special parts of the *retina* in your eye, see colours. These parts are called *cones*. Other parts of the retina see darkness and lightness. These parts are called *rods*. Rods tell you about the shapes of objects.

There are three types of cones in your eyes. Each type of cone is sensitive to a particular range of colours around red, green and blue.

Cones need more light to work than rods do. So you can see shapes of things in moonlight, but not colours. Try it out tonight.

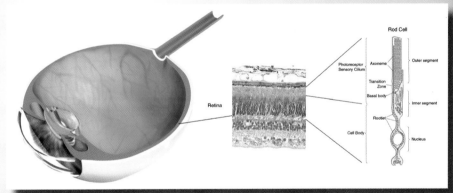

The vanishing colour

You will need:

• a red piece of paper

1. Hold the red piece of paper in front of you. Fix your eyes on a spot just beyond the paper.

2. Slowly move your arm to the side, keeping your eyes on the spot in front. Is there a point at which you can still see the paper, but not its colour? Actually, there are fewer cones at the sides of your eyes. So the colour of the object fades out.

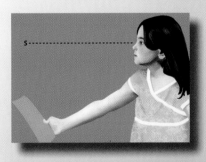

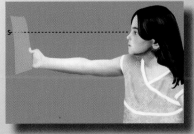

Optical Illusions

I am sure you believe your own eyes. But be careful; sometimes your eyes may appear to see something which is not really there. This is called an optical illusion. In fact, your eyes do see correctly, but your brain interprets the messages from your eyes incorrectly.

Is this a perfect square? View it from the top. Then raise the book to your eye level and look at the square diagonally.

Are the two vertical lines straight? Which of the two horizontal lines is longer?

How many cubes do you see?

Turn the book and count again.

What is this?

Is this a picture of a trophy, or two men facing each other?

Look at this strange sight. A duck with a nose ring. Wait a second! I thought it was a lady rabbit showing off her new earring!

Funny fingers

1. Put your two forefingers together and hold them about three inches in front of your eyes, as shown in the picture. Look over the fingers and focus your eyes on something far away.
2. Now hold your fingers a little away from each other and look between them.
   What do you see? Compare it with the figure given on the side.

When you hold your two fingers in front of your eyes, the image of your left finger in your left eye and the image of your right finger in your right eye come together in part, and you see a funny finger with a nail at each end!

A fish in a bowl

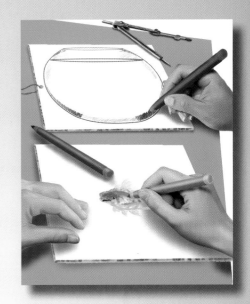

You will need:

- a 2-inch square cardboard
- crayons
- a pencil
- thread

1. Take the cardboard and make two holes in it. Tie short pieces of string as shown in picture.
2. Draw a large fish-bowl on one side of the cardboard and a small fish on the other side.
3. Hold the pieces of string between your fingers. Now turn the cardboard very fast with your fingers. What do you see? Turn the page to know why this happens.

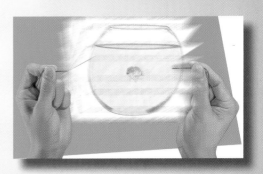

Your eyes can keep the image of a thing for about half a second after you have put that thing away. When the cardboard turns fast enough your eyes see the fish and the fish-bowl at the same time, and you see a fish in the bowl!

Did you know that this is the basic idea behind motion pictures or movies? A film consists of a series of pictures, each slightly different from the last one. When shown fast enough, we get an impression of movement. You can verify this.

You will need:

- a paper and a pencil
- an exercise book

1. Draw figure 1 at the top corner of the first page of the exercise book, figure 2 at the top corner of the 2nd page and so on till the 16th page.
2. Flip the pages fast. What do you see?

After-images

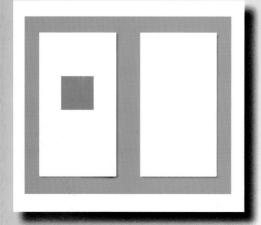

1. Draw a 1-inch square on the first sheet of white paper. Colour it red. Look at it steadily while slowly counting up to 30. Then look at the other white sheet. What do you notice?
2. Do the same experiment with the other colours. The coloured image that you saw on the white paper is called an *after-image*. While you were staring at the red square, the cones of your eyes sensitive to red light got tired. So when you looked away, only the green and blue cones were active and you saw a greenish blue square!

The effect of after-images can be more startling in the bird-in-a-cage experiment.

1. Draw a picture of a bird on all three coloured papers. Cut out the birds. Mark their eyes with the pen.
2. Paste them on the three cards.
3. On the fourth card draw a cage.
4. Place the cards in a well-lit area. Stare at the red bird for 20 seconds and then quickly look at the cage. What do you see?
5. Repeat the process with the green bird and then the blue bird. Did you see a yellow bird when you stared at the blue one? Why?